BABY CHICKENS

by Martha London

Cody Koala
An Imprint of Pop!
popbooksonline.com

abdobooks.com
Published by Pop!, a division of ABDO, PO Box 398166, Minneapolis, Minnesota 55439.

Printed in the United States of America, North Mankato, Minnesota

052020
092020

THIS BOOK CONTAINS RECYCLED MATERIALS

Cover Photo: Shutterstock Images
Interior Photos: Shutterstock Images, 1, 5 (top), 5 (bottom left), 5 (bottom right), 6, 9, 10, 13, 14–15, 19 (top), 19 (bottom left), 19 (bottom right), 20; iStockphoto, 17

Editor: Nick Rebman
Series Designer: Christine Ha

Library of Congress Control Number: 2019954952

Publisher's Cataloging-in-Publication Data
Names: London, Martha, author.
Title: Baby chickens / by Martha London
Description: Minneapolis, Minnesota : POP!, 2021 | Series: Baby farm animals | Includes online resources and index
Identifiers: ISBN 9781532167423 (lib. bdg.) | ISBN 9781532168529 (ebook)
Subjects: LCSH: Chickens--Infancy--Juvenile literature. | Chicks--Juvenile literature. | Baby chicks--Juvenile literature. | Baby birds--Juvenile literature. | Baby farm animals--Juvenile literature. | Animal babies--Juvenile literature.
Classification: DDC 636.2--dc23

Hello! My name is

Cody Koala

Pop open this book and you'll find QR codes like this one, loaded with information, so you can learn even more!

Scan this code* and others like it while you read, or visit the website below to make this book pop.

popbooksonline.com/baby-chickens

*Scanning QR codes requires a web-enabled smart device with a QR code reader app and a camera.

Table of Contents

Chapter 1

Breaking Out

Baby chickens are called chicks. Chicks are birds. They **hatch** from eggs. They use their beaks to peck their shells. The shells break apart.

Watch a video here!

Chicks have soft, fluffy feathers called **down**. The mother chicken is called a hen. She keeps her chicks warm. She covers the chicks with her wings.

There are more than 25 billion chickens in the world.

Chapter 2

Safe and Warm

Chicks need a warm, dry place to live. Many farmers put their chicks in an indoor **brood** box. The brood box keeps chicks safe.

Complete an activity here!

eye
beak
down
foot

Young chicks are too small to go outside. Other animals could eat them. But after a few weeks, farmers let the chicks outside. The chicks start to explore.

Chickens keep themselves clean by taking dust baths.

Chapter 3

From Peep to Cluck

Chicks **molt** when they are three to six weeks old. They lose their fluffy **down**. They grow their adult feathers. These feathers keep the chicks warm and dry.

Learn more here!

Chickens reach their adult size when they are six months old. Male chickens are called roosters. They can **crow** loudly. Roosters usually have brighter feathers than hens.

Many farmers put their chickens in coops. A coop keeps chickens safe from **predators**. Farmers put food and water in the coop. Chickens eat feed. It is made up of grains and small bits of meat.

Chapter 4

Flock Together

Farmers raise chickens for eggs and meat. Some kinds of chickens lay more eggs than others. Certain chickens can lay up to 300 eggs per year.

Learn more here!

Some kinds of chickens grow quickly. Farmers keep these chickens for meat. Farmers sell male chickens when they are big enough. Farmers sell hens for meat when they are done laying eggs.

Making Connections

Text-to-Self

If you were a farmer, would you keep chickens on your farm? Why or why not?

Text-to-Text

Have you read other books about farm animals? How are chickens similar to and different from those animals?

Text-to-World

There are many chickens in the world. Why do you think chickens are so common?

Glossary

brood – a group of young birds hatched and cared for at one time.

crow – to make a loud call.

down – the soft feathers that chicks are born with.

hatch – to be born from an egg.

molt – to lose old feathers and grow new ones.

predator – an animal that hunts other animals for food.

Index

Online Resources

popbooksonline.com

Thanks for reading this Cody Koala book!

Scan this code* and others like it in this book, or visit the website below to make this book pop!

popbooksonline.com/baby-chickens

*Scanning QR codes requires a web-enabled smart device with a QR code reader app and a camera.